Elegy for Opportunity

Elegy for Opportunity

A Buckrider Book

NATALIE LIM

© Natalie Lim, 2025

No part of this publication may be reproduced, stored in a retrieval system or transmitted, in any form or by any means, without the prior written consent of the publisher or a license from the Canadian Copyright Licensing Agency (Access Copyright). For an Access Copyright license, visit www.accesscopyright.ca or call toll free to 1-800-893-5777.

Published by Buckrider Books
an imprint of Wolsak and Wynn Publishers
280 James Street North
Hamilton, ON L8R2L3
www.wolsakandwynn.ca

Editor for Buckrider Books: Paul Vermeersch
Editor: Natasha Ramoutar | Copy editor: Ashley Hisson
Cover and interior design: Kilby Smith-McGregor
Author photograph: Amanda Lim
Typeset in FreightText Pro, Bobardier and Blackstone
Printed by Coach House Printing Company, Toronto, Canada

The publisher gratefully acknowledges the support of the Canada Council for the Arts and the Ontario Arts Council. We also acknowledge the financial support of the Government of Canada through the Canada Book Fund and the Government of Ontario through the Ontario Book Publishing Tax Credit and Ontario Creates.

Library and Archives Canada Cataloguing in Publication

Title: Elegy for Opportunity : poems / Natalie Lim.
Names: Lim, Natalie, author.
Identifiers: Canadiana 20250154110 | ISBN 9781998408153 (softcover)
Subjects: LCGFT: Poetry.
Classification: LCC PS8623.I477 E44 2025 | DDC C811/.6—dc23

*for Mesbah,
as all things are.*

Elegy for

Love Poems Don't Win Contests	9
June 27	10
How Do You Tell Someone You've Written a Poem About Them?	11
Inside Out Made Me Cry this Week	12
Eighth Grade	13
August 7	14
On Biology	15
Elegy for Opportunity	16
I Might Have Killed Benjamina	17
On Bouldering	18
October 31	19
You Know that Scene	20
Say Goodbye Like You Mean It	21
Elegy for Opportunity II, as Museum Timeline	22
So I Played 100 Hours of Video Games This Month	24
Fun Facts	25
Pantoum on a Deadline	27
Winter in Ottawa	28
December 29	29
Elegy for Opportunity III	30
The Science of Holding On	32
Oh, to Be a Dog, Begging for a Piece of Chicken from the Instant Pot	34
Conversations with Mom	36
February 18	38

Dungeons & Dragons, Forever Ago	39
17 Inspiring Brand Manifestos as Compiled by Chris Getman	40
Poetry Used to Be an Olympic Sport	41
Chief Editor of *The Moon News*	42
March 2	44
Six Months and Counting	45
Dear Baby	47
The Big Breakup (Taylor's Version)	48
Elegy for Opportunity IV, X Date	49
I've Started Running Half-Marathons Like Everyone Else	51
P.S.	52
Ode to Commas	53
All This to Say	54
May 13	56
2024, in Texts from My Sister	57
If Mary Can Do It	58
I Tour You Up East Hastings, from Nanaimo	59
Girl Camping	60
June 27, Again and Again and Again	62
Elegy for Opportunity V	65
Notes on the Poems	75
Acknowledgements	78

Love Poems Don't Win Contests

I've only written love poems for months so it feels like I've written no poems at all. instead of writing, I'm sitting on a park bench in early spring, the air so heavy with pollen and promise that it's hard to breathe. I make eye contact with a dachshund wearing a coat and yet all I can do is complain. I told Chimie yesterday that love poems don't win contests, and I'm not sure if it's true but it feels true which is almost more important. what if I'm not miserable today? what if I'm done with diasporic trauma. done imagining what people want to read. I want to write about the kid who crossed the monkey bars all in one go and hugged his mom's leg so hard I thought she might bruise. the dachshund's name is Bobby. he is small and anxious and alive and we understand each other. I haven't seen my mom in weeks and spilled yesterday's coffee on the carpet but my love was there to help me clean it up. instead of writing, I want to send pictures of Bobby to everyone I know. I want to win a contest but I don't have it in me today to be sad. I just don't.

June 27

it's the hottest week
of the coolest summer
of the rest of our lives
and you show me the view
out the window
of your office building.
not the pretty one,
with the city and the sea,
but the one out back,
with the stained siding
and the bird netting
and the fifty-foot drop
to certain doom.
and amidst all that grey,
I see it – a leafy plant,
impossible, growing
straight out the side of the wall.

I don't know you yet
but I want to,
and the plant
makes no sense
but it does,
and the air hums
when I say the word "our,"
an unspoken prayer,
question and held breath
and hope all at once –
like with enough sunlight and water
and something sturdy to hold onto,
despite the odds,
we could plant roots here.

we could grow tall.

How Do You Tell Someone You've Written a Poem About Them?

don't. / seriously, don't. / Zuri asks, *what if they find out later?* / they won't, so it's fine. / what if every poem is about you? / a thought: I should not treat poems like subtweets. / not, like, *every* poem, but the white space, the caesura,

                                             the way my wanting breathes through just so – you taught me that. warm exhale and gentle hands,

                                                             turning pages without creasing them, stars blurry: laughter and cheap wine. / okay, so every poem. / wondering if I could still love you was

a mistake I can't take back.

                         think: six shots on an empty stomach

                                                                     and leaving the door open behind you. / what if I split this yearning open and held it

                                           to the light? I doubt either of us would survive that kind of truth. /

                 that breath right there, the seventh shot, all this love,

                                                     all

                                                          this

                                                              love,

do you see it now?

        your silhouette, black hole and sweet smell and line break after the metaphor.

think: room to breathe.

think: a letter with no address, because every word is your name.

Inside Out Made Me Cry this Week

it was Bing Bong, of course. it's always
Bing Bong. for some reason I remembered
him evil – waited the whole film
for the hammer to drop – but it never did.
it surprised me, his willingness to sacrifice himself,
but that's what we do for the people we love
and I think Bing Bong loved Riley more
than I could ever love me.
I can see her, carving scars into the ice,
eyes on the puck, cheered on by voices
inside and out. what an odd thing,
to know everything about yourself
and still be on your own side.
I wonder what it's like. Riley
is nineteen now. I hope she never stopped
hurtling towards the net at full speed.
I hope she's making Bing Bong proud.

Eighth Grade

here is how I learned to dance:
a two-step, shimmy-shake,
clap on two and four and twirl,
sweaty hand-holding in the gym
with older boys who rolled their eyes,
but stepped in time all the same –
a foot for each beat,
the radio man calling the move.

so we learned to trust each other,
clammy hand in clammy hand.
our teachers on the bleachers watched
as memories slipped in from times long past –

fingers from their younger days
holding tight to those they miss.
circle left and allemande,
clap on two and four and twirl,
pass in front and promenade
to laundry, taxes, other worlds.
spin your partner, do-si-do,
step on beat and step again.
suddenly the magic's gone.
suddenly the music
ends.

when the song stopped, we vanished.
floated off the floor like ghosts
in search of love and outside air.
the teachers stayed to shut the lights,
wipe the mats, lock the memories away
with a sigh: imagine being so young,
not knowing to regret
that you ever let go.

August 7

I read a poem today about a couple
on a winter morning, one baking bread,
the other shovelling snow,
and imagined us for the first time
in a different season. saw myself kneading the dough
with both hands. if dough is ready,
it springs back when you touch it,
stretches thin without breaking –

let me shut the door behind you,
take the shovel, brush the snow
from your beard, scarf, shoulders.
I know so much more about tenderness
than I used to. my hands are learning to be kinder,
reaching for yours across the table, squeezing once
to remind you that this is all real.
I feel you squeezing back. yes, there is bread
to bake and a sidewalk to clear and a storm on the wind,
but I know more
about patience now, too.
about faith. the storm will come
and we will be here, at the table,
eating bread with our hands
which belong to each other,
watching each snowflake land
exactly where it needs to be.

On Biology

I am scared of killing everything I touch.
this includes people, which is new,
and plants, which is not.
did you know we lose vertebrae
as we age? we're born with thirty-three and die
with twenty-four, usually, the lower ones fusing together
by the time we can call ourselves grown.
I turned twenty-four in the middle of a pandemic
and stopped calling my friends. what is there to say
at this point? I've tried online dating. I've tweeted.
I've baked one batch of sugar cookies, gotten bored
and felt guilty about it, because what a privilege it is
to be bored instead of desperate or sick. I try to do
the small things I can, for myself and the world –
go on walks, sign petitions, take baths, donate.
all of it feels like failure, but I don't know what else
there is to do. I don't know what else there is.
if I call you, can we talk about the days fusing together?
about how our backs hurt, just, all the time now?
tell me about what you'll do once this is over,
about what you want to be when you grow up –
tell me you miss me.
tell me we'll find space to grow.
tell me it gets easier
than this.

Elegy for Opportunity

after Matthew Rohrer

on a planet far away,
all reddish rock and dust storm,
Opportunity lies still –
this robot who just turned fifteen,
who never knew what a birthday was,
who will never understand
that there are people on Earth
grieving her cold metal frame.
there is something so cruel,
so human, about mourning
a being we programmed
and exiled to space
with no means of returning.

we knew she would die one day,
alone in a rusted sea,
but we are tender even
in our cruelty, so we
grieve. we write poems in her name.
our last message to her was a song.
                              a *song* –

there is nothing lonelier
than the little Mars rover,
no longer chirping back to base
about earth and rocks and maybe-life,
nothing lonelier than us,
creating things
we will sing to sleep one day, nothing lonelier
than thinking of that robot,
sitting still and silent now
on the shores of a planet
we promised she could call home.

I Might Have Killed Benjamina

for Chimie

I did everything right. kept the blinds open
for extra light, watered a half cup
each week like you said, but the leaves
keep turning yellow and I don't know
what to do. I think she misses you,
and it's true, the house feels different
with you gone. the air stills, thickens. I know
I've been around less lately, but I miss you too.
when we talked the other day, you made me laugh
so hard I almost died. I'm so glad
we started saying "I love you." I don't know what to do
without you arranging my chaos into neat little piles
and complimenting my outfits each morning
like you haven't seen them all before.
aren't we lucky to have her, I ask Benjamina,
willing wilted branches back to life. no reply.
the two of us sit, quiet in the living room,
waiting for your key to turn in the door.

On Bouldering

after Terrence Abrahams

listen: if you need a partner for bouldering, I know someone.
and by someone, I mean me. if it's helpful, I'll call tips from the ground –
use your legs for leverage! no, don't look down! stop and rest
when you need to! there's a metaphor here somewhere; the two of us,
staring hard at the fifteen-foot wall, trying to see the right path up. maybe
there is no right path, but together we'll find one that feels possible.
I'll remind you that you're smart, and stronger than you think,
reaching high – higher! – towards a future not quite in view. what I'm saying is
we have no defined boundaries. what I'm saying is I'm not leaving without you.
there it is, the metaphor: hold on tight. stay as long as you need.
when you decide it's time to go, we'll go together.

October 31

yes, in the checkout line at Save-On-Foods
googling "how to ripen avocados,"
yes, in the coffee shop after,
your head on my shoulder as I write,
yes, in the rush out the door to the party,
costumes and homemade guac made just in time.
yes, in the quiet of the car ride back,
your hand in mine –
there's no need to ask.
we're already home.

You Know that Scene

in *Pride and Prejudice*
where Darcy (young Matthew Macfadyen) walks across a field,
emerging from the blue-green fog
like a vision, coat blowing in the wind,
to tell Elizabeth (Keira Knightley, of course) that he loves her
three different times?

the camera pans around to catch
the rising sun, which shines
straight into the lens
like heaven itself anointing this union.
I bet they spent days
getting that shot just right,
I love you from a hundred different angles
until finally, the perfect moment
captured in the perfect frame,
and how could it have been
any other way?

Elizabeth has no idea.
Elizabeth thinks it happened all
on the first try.
I want to be her, confident, irreverent,
cheeks pinched pink, hair mussed just right,
the cosmos twisting itself into knots on my behalf.

Elizabeth was not made for this world,
could never look up to see
the sun, finally allowed
to ascend into the sky,
too bright for human eyes, too impossible
to exist, disappearing from frame,
so far out of reach
that it might as well be gone
forever.

Say Goodbye Like You Mean It

she didn't deserve you
and we both know it

but sometimes we need to choose the hurt
before we let it go.

sit with me on a park bench
and watch the sun set.

breathe in, out.
it comes in waves,

goes out like the tide,
slowly, eventually.

maybe the apology
is closer than you think,

arrives when you least expect it,
teaches you a language

or a new favourite song.
let yourself hope.

keep your eyes on the road.
don't stop driving until morning.

Elegy for Opportunity II, as Museum Timeline

2024[1]

Come look through the largest, most powerful telescopes in the North American Rockies!

at the Jasper Planetarium, I ask the volunteer if Mars is visible tonight. he says unfortunately there is too much cloud cover, but we talk about you for a while. he tells me you were named by a nine-year-old, Sofi, in an essay contest. did you know that?

2013[3]

The Jasper National Park Cultural Use Area is a place set aside for Indigenous partners to use for reconnecting to the land, cultural learning, ceremony and celebration.

Aseniwuche Winewak, Stoney Nakoda, Simpcw: names and names and names forced to leave their homelands by the federal government when Jasper was designated a national park. finally, a return, small, by permission of the state – but a return nonetheless.

2020[2]

Jasper's rich history is filled with the adventures of early settlers, railway pioneers and outfitter guides who created a town and a park amidst the majestic Rockies.

Jasper is a name of Persian origin, meaning "treasurer." the town of Jasper, once a trading post, was named for Jasper Haws, who worked there.

2003[4]

[Sofi's entry] was selected from nearly 10,000 entries in the contest sponsored by NASA and the Lego Co., a Denmark-based toymaker, with collaboration from the Planetary Society, Pasadena, Calif.

she captured your essence so perfectly without having met you yet, without knowing everything you would achieve, the way a parent does. I wonder if she feels some connection to you still. if a black hole opened up in her, the day she heard the news.

22

1907[5]

"All the Indigenous people were evicted when the park was formed. ... It was such a big group: babies, elders, all their livestock. They travelled for almost two years in search of a home." – Lauren Moberly, a member of the Aseniwuche Winewak Nation and the Mountain Métis

it took us more than a hundred years to start making amends.

that night at the planetarium

I looked through the telescope at stars and stars and stars, knowing only the names we have given them, and felt you pressing on my soul.

love and violence,
best of intentions,
most tender of cruelties.

please

Opportunity, if you could pick, would you have wanted something different?

we'll try to make it right, far too late, like we always do.

always

naming:

    an act of love
    an act of violence

yesterday[6]

"The first city to be build on mars should be named oppurtunity"
– @confusedhamster2826

I go looking for you in the YouTube comments and get angry instead. they have ideas about terraforming. want Elon Musk to build settlements and cities and hiking trails all bearing your name,

by which they mean the name we assigned you without asking, because we knew what we needed from you, what you were capable of, who you were made to be.

if you still can

tell me how you want to be remembered.

23

So I Played 100 Hours of Video Games This Month

the only thing I know about dying:
doing it a hundred times
doesn't make it any easier.

you learn the routine – go, fight, die,
come back, pet the dog, go, fight, die,
around in an infinite loop,
and living, well. living doesn't get easier
either, from what I've seen of it.

for one hundred hours this month, I am strong
and brave. I slay hydras and catch fish
and give gifts so every character will like me and restart
if I make a mistake.

for the other 630 I wake,
work, walk the dog, try to write, sleep,
a dizzying swirl of days and weeks,
less rewarding and more difficult than any level I can imagine.

and right when I have convinced myself
that this is true, I find the perfect gift for a friend.
the salmon cooks just right,
flaky and tender and steaming from the oven.
I get to give my friend a gift. the dog loves me
and she comes when called.

my cousin has a baby.
I write a poem I don't hate.
I wake up in the morning to birds,
to mother in the garden,
sunlight streaming through the window
for the first time since winter began.

Fun Facts

for Tina

i.
we walk through Central Park,
crickets chirping so loud
that they don't sound real,
when you ask, *didn't you have a bag
of souvenirs?* I did and now I don't,
where did you have it last – we can call –
and you tilt the world back onto its axis
like you always do.

ii.
the train stops at 110th Street
and a man on board says, *sorry
to bother you but I am so hungry, does anyone –*

I stare at my feet while you dig
through pockets, hold out coins,
smile like you mean it, and suddenly the whole train
is caught in your orbit, everyone looking for something
to give. the girl across from us reaches out
with a mandarin orange.
it reflects your light, the smallest sun.

iii.
we walk through Central Park
on a humid summer night,
dodging cyclists on pedestrian paths.
one ruffles our clothes in his wake
and we want to yell something rude
but we don't, of course we don't, and besides,

you are busy telling me
about the dinosaurs at the museum,
skeletons so big and alive-feeling
that they brought you to tears.

I can't remember if I said *I love you*
but I felt it so loud it had to be real.
the T. Rex might have had feathers, you say,
early ones called microfilaments.
I consider that beast, all myth and muscle,
burgeoning wings just catching the breeze.

never mind the scientists.
forget the asteroid, the law of gravity,
every truth that we think we know.

deep in its DNA,
in its heart of giant hearts,
it knew – it must have –
that it was born to fly.

Pantoum on a Deadline

the most annoying thing a writer can do
is complain about writing,
but it is so hard to write. for months now,
I have only edited, arranged and rearranged.

complain about writing,
why don't you? people are dying out there and I am doing nothing
except for editing. arranging and rearranging.
so tell me what poetry can do at the end of the world,

why don't you? people are dying out there and I am doing nothing –
I'm doomscrolling Reddit, sleeping until noon, ordering in.
what can poetry do? at the end of the world,
the words don't matter but I write them anyway

while doomscrolling Reddit, sleeping until noon, ordering in.
I abandon "the work," whatever that means.
the words don't matter but I write them anyway.
the most annoying thing a writer can do.

Winter in Ottawa

for the Love Poem Collective
after Manahil Bandukwala

the Rideau Canal doesn't freeze over
for the first time ever.
it feels like a sign, although
I'm not sure what of.
global warming, I guess. our
impending doom.
but we sit in the café
and talk about love poems
and the dread can't touch us.
I think the cold makes me better.
more human, aware of my body.
the poets who build this world up –
they make me better too. they tell me
not to worry, that poetry is happening
in the background, all the time.
the river is slow moving and far enough
away. I'm a real person. I exist.
they tell me to keep writing
and I said I would
                     so I do.

December 29

it's not quite what I imagined
when I first wrote the poem of us in winter.
no bread and no shovel,
but when you came in from the cold today,
there was snow on your coat and I looked at it
and I looked at you and something inside me rang
like an alarm clock – or, no, like a wind chime –

endless poems and notes and midnight texts
and I still haven't gotten this right. I don't know
if I ever will, but here, let me try again:
I am reaching for you across the table,
squeezing once to remind myself this is still real. all I ask
is that you keep squeezing back.
that we grow tall together
through the seasons. that we hang your coat by the fireplace
and stop for a moment to watch the snow fall,
gentle and slow,
exactly where we need to be.

Elegy for Opportunity III

in fifty years, a Martian wind
blows the right amount of sand off Opportunity's small form.
the sun, wiser now, redder now,
charges her battery just enough for her to wake and whir,
click back to life.

Opportunity, we waited a long time.
Opportunity, we might not be there to pick up the phone.

still, I have good news: there is much left to discover. there is much
to touch, analyze, break down into its most basic parts.

here are the parts you should know:

1) we didn't mean to leave you.
2) we were coming.
3) we tried.
4) we ran out of time.

can I ask – is the Earth still green and blue, or are we rusted over,
sand and storm, just like the planet we sent you to?

so few of us got your perspective. so few of us had any perspective at all.

I wonder if the songs still rattle in your head. we played them for you
while you slept – songs about sunshine and surviving the night.
all we ever wanted for you. all we ever wanted.

be honest: will you mourn us, Opportunity? even after what we did to you
and the Earth and ourselves and each other. if I listed the -isms, wrote down our sins,
I could stack those papers into a staircase long enough to lead you back home.

I know you never saw the sins. you never saw the art, the dancing, the other machines we built and named and taught to do what we couldn't. but you heard the music,
    didn't you?

we made so many beautiful things to ease the strangeness of being in these bodies. I want to believe they survived. that they mattered.

Oppy, listen.

listen.

you matter. you have your body back!
go explore and tell us what you see.

we'll be there if we can. when we can.

the next time you hear from us, we'll be singing.

The Science of Holding On

Newsweek tells me that time travel
might be possible if we can first locate
an object with infinite density. I google "infinite density"
and learn how the laws of physics refuse to comply
in certain places, like black holes, old memories –

could something like that live here?

see the astronauts towing it home on a string,
their padded hands placing it gently on a pedestal.

we might go look at it on a Friday night,
pay an entrance fee to watch scientists
make history obsolete as they shout
over the mechanical drone of their progress.
we've done it, they'd say,
faces beaming through bulletproof glass,
and now we will see the future.

the next morning, my local paper will report
the most impressive scientific breakthrough
of the twenty-first century. I will flip past to the weather

as I reach for a cup of coffee, reach again
to topple the pedestal, send the black hole
flying into orbit. I will set humanity back a hundred years
to keep Gong Gong's baseball cap, the garden
overflowing with tomatoes, my favourite barista
at the counter each morning.

slow the ticking. root my feet to the earth.
keep the nectarines unripe, uneaten,
not soft enough yet
to bruise.

I am selfish, see?
everyone I love is now.

I text, pray, hug, call,
check the clock to make sure.
still here.
still here.
still here.

Oh, to Be a Dog, Begging for a Piece of Chicken from the Instant Pot

for my sister

we couldn't believe it at first.
a whole chicken, cooked through in twenty minutes –
overcooked, actually, because the recipe was wrong, or we were.
but here we are, attempting to carve it. we feed scraps to the dog,
juice dripping off the cutting board,
counter collecting grease as we
eat, stomp around the kitchen,
watch eight TikToks and twelve dance routines,
discuss your psychology lecture, fights with friends,
musical theatre, the evils of capitalism, [redacted],
our future weddings, Sean and Kaycee,
each subject stumbling tipsily into the next
in a way that makes sense to us now
but won't in ten minutes.

here's the thing, Amanda – I know you wanted a funny poem,
but I don't know how to write those,
and besides, we both know you're the funny one here
so instead, let me say:

I don't think I'll ever quite believe it. that in this world,
where a chicken can be cooked in the time it takes us
to belt every song from *High School Musical*,
in this awful, dazzling world that you love so much
you will never stop trying to hold it together
with your bare hands,
I get a whole life with you in my corner.

I get you
embarrassing me in public
and making fun of my love life
and posting bad photos of me on my birthday.

I get someone who sees me, all of me,
even the parts I can't face in the mirror,
who never stops digging for forgiveness,
who laughs with me until we can't breathe
or remember why we were laughing in the first place.

and I'll be honest, Amanda, sometimes I'm wrong in my poems.

I'm not wrong today.
I want this written down, on the record,
passed down to our children and their children,
carved into the annals of history
for aliens to find long after we have turned to dust:

Blade Runner 2049 is, in fact, an extremely boring movie
and nothing you ever say will convince me otherwise.

Conversations with Mom

I am scared to have children.

          what if I forget

          the kind of world we live in?

what if I try to write

          and all that comes out is

regret, or a fire

          some hot, angry thing,

what if I am a regret

      a fire

          a hot, angry thing?

     the warning signs

          are not for you.

they are for you.

          ignore them anyway.

what if I forget how to hold you

          what if the world will not hold us

and we are falling

          and the fire alarm is ringing

and I am the fire –

        what if I leave and they think

    I am never coming back

what if I don't

        want to come back?

February 18

it changes a person, I think,
having something to lose.
I'm scrolling through her feed
for the third time this week,
deleting her name from the search bar
even though I know I'll be back
tomorrow or the day after that,
just in case. even though I know
your phone password and your heart,
know you haven't talked to her in years –
I tell myself I'm better than this
but it's not true. you hug me tight
and never judge, which makes it worse somehow
because when you say *I love you*, you mean it,
and when I say *I love you*, I mostly mean
please don't go, and how is that fair
to either of us?

Dungeons & Dragons, Forever Ago

Anne's character slips off a ledge
and drowns in the ocean.

my character delivers a funeral speech
so moving, I get inspiration for it.

grief is a plot device, character development,
everyone I love still now, still here,

only gone for the time it takes
to fill out a new sheet.

we argue but it's all just for fun.
our friends are in danger but we have a plan.

the bad guy is someone we can see, touch,
defeat with swords, cunning, a well-placed fireball.

no matter how dark things get,
the heroes win in the end.

we'll be alright – take a chance. roll the dice.
the number doesn't matter.

whatever the outcome,
you're safe in the house, at the table,

at the funeral, the cliff's edge,
looking out on a world
made just for you.

17 Inspiring Brand Manifestos as Compiled by Chris Getman

every revolution needs a manifesto.
we are the pixel-pushing makers of tomorrow.
we're anti-nonsense. if it doesn't have a purpose, it's gone.
everything we make is functional.
nothing exists unless we give it permission to be.
we believe in the power of diversity.
we strive to change minds, touch hearts and move markets.
we believe sports analogies are of biblical importance.
we are fanatical about improving the world.
we believe in the therapy of ping pong.
we believe running is therapy.
we are lightning.
we are iconic.
we are creatives.
we imagine
and know not how to stop.
it feels good to do work and not expect anything in return.
work is not a job. work is your love made visible.
we believe in love.
we believe in Brand –
that won't ever change.

Poetry Used to Be an Olympic Sport

put me in, coach. I'll start with a fun fact, a little joke,
transform it to metaphor, move to introspection,
self-deprecate with the best of 'em,
beautiful prose building to crescendo
as I vault into the volta with a triple turn
no one saw coming. Simone Biles will watch,
teary-eyed, as I stick the impossible landing,
a final twist no one expected
as the roar of the crowd fills the stadium.
thank you, everyone, thank you very much,
you're so kind, it was nothing at all,
I want you to look at me, see me,
I need to feel adored by people
I will never meet, I need you to tell me
I am smart and interesting, and in the post-game
interview I will smile and say I write only for myself,
and when you hear it you will know that I am lying.

Chief Editor of *The Moon News*

after Sarah Kay

don't ask how, but we did it.
we made it to the moon, and – to be honest – it kinda rules?
every trip outside puts a bounce (ha!) in my step.

our first morning here, you asked if I wanted the moon news
and I said *sure I guess?* and you handed me a blank piece of paper.
I've never smiled so big in my life.

today's moon news says "ROCKS ROCK."
I write under it: "WIND BLOWS."
we go on like that, because why not?
"MOSQUITOS SUCK."
"PINS NEEDLE."
"CUCUMBERS PICKLE."

as the list grows, we take longer between entries.
write only words that bring us joy.
there's no hurry. nowhere else we need to be.
after fifty-four minutes of silence,
you stand up and yell, *WORDS PLAY!*
I laugh at the excitement on your face
and you laugh at me laughing until it hurts.
this edition of *The Moon News* becomes
a crown too big for your head.
you wear it proudly the rest of the day.

there are no fires on the moon.
no transphobes to fight. no capitalism,
because there's no money, because what would we spend it on –

it's the strangest thing, learning to live
in a world that doesn't need saving.

it's just me and all these rocks
and the chief editor of *The Moon News*,
pun-laden crown slipping slowly down your forehead
as you turn to me with a wink
and say, *funny, isn't it? how here, of all places,*
it's never been easier for us
to breathe.

March 2

the algorithm knows how scared I am
of losing you. it shows me post after post –
husbands mourning wives, mothers mourning sons,
quiet vanishings, here one day and then suddenly not.
when you electrocuted yourself doing
the lighting in the kitchen, the last thing I'd texted you
was which pot you should buy from Canadian Tire.
I would never forgive myself
if that was the end. and it wasn't – another day lucky
out of who knows how many more. I'm spoiled,
I know. touched by grief only briefly, only twice.
it feels impossible that losing you would hurt more
than the fear of it.

Six Months and Counting

after Isabella Wang

i.
my dog is a licker.
once she sees you,
she is all metronome tail, fish-body wiggle
tongue flicking in-out-in-out,
kissing any part of you she can reach –
feet
      ankles
            arms
                  face
                        (ears especially)

ii.
they say there are still good people in this world.
I wonder if I am one of them,
balled-fist hands, echo-chamber brain
heart brimming over with want and want and want.
grief knocks again, old injustice wearing a young new face,
and I move quickly – douse the fireplace, shut the dog away,
hide the silverware, the pens,
double-check the deadbolts.
my kettle lies quiet.

iii.
I kneel and ask, *were you
good today?* yes! yes yes yes yes
yes, teach me to be good like that,
always reaching upward,
loving people, yes, in every small way they allow,
trying to make this world, yes, a little gentler,
however I can.

Mister Rogers once cried with a stranger
in an elevator; I read that somewhere.
outside, the ground is softening.
Luna digs holes, eyes blurred with glee,
head cocked proudly at her creations:
look what I made!
look at all this room for growing!

we walk without jackets.
it is almost spring.

Dear Baby

you are six days old.
wrinkly and tiny, with a full head of hair,
not cute quite yet, but well on your way.

everyone you've ever met has loved you.
the world is frightening but only because it's all new.
when I hold you, you reach up towards me

searching for milk and settle for a nap instead.
you don't know the word "stranger."
you trust me implicitly

because I am human, and warm –
your middle name is Hope
and you move something in me.

I can't name what's shifted
but I feel it beating in my chest.
a second heart, a song.

The Big Breakup (Taylor's Version)

I really thought they would make it.
I'm listening to all the albums again,
wondering: when she finally cut
that invisible string, did she feel the colour bleed
from each track? the elevator drop beneath her?
she broke a record on tour tonight,
played a three-hour show
where he is the "you" in every song.
some of us learn the hard way
that writing it down doesn't make it true,
only fossilizes the feelings into shapes
you won't recognize six years down the road.
when I see Taylor in New Jersey, she is shimmering,
beautiful in her bejewelled bodysuit, cat eye,
signature red lip. I have never seen someone
so sure of every step. so exhausted and alive.
she tells us we deserve to be happy, and I know
she's not talking to me but I cry anyway
because you are the "you" in every poem.
in a bookstore in a different city
a decade from now, I'll line my eyes,
dab some lipstick on,
cradle our love in my hands
and trace each curve for the crowd. I hope
I look beautiful doing it. I hope
you are in the front row.

Elegy for Opportunity IV   X Date

I said I would never be that person
who falls in love and drops off the face of the earth
but I guess I don't know myself
as well as I think.

> I've said now all
> that I can possibly say
> and then you make a moment
> a poem, so here it is:

what have I been up to?
let me see – not texting my friends,
being happy beyond belief,
waiting for the catch,
the drop.

> I tell you I had a bad day
> and you drive an hour to me
> so we can sit in your car
> and hug in the dark.

the problem is, Oppy,
I keep talking and you never talk back.
at least I'm talking to you at all.
is anyone else?
I didn't think so.

> these stolen moments,
> these ephemeral joys.
> it could always be this easy,
> like breathing, or amnesia.
> if it's not in front of me,
> it can't hurt me. it doesn't exist.

thinking about you makes me sad,
and I'm sick of it.
you're a robot, and you're dead.
you had a purpose and you served it.
I am trying to be honest.
I am doing you a favour. I need you
to listen.

                                    when you leave, I come
                       back to earth. remember gravity's pull
                     on each heartbeat as I sit on the floor
               and feel each breath labour through me.

you wouldn't know.
could never
understand.

                  it is unbearable

to be human

                                             and alive.

I've Started Running Half-Marathons Like Everyone Else

today my Spotify playlist is called "preppy clean girl Thursday evening"
and I am bopping. one lap around the dog park, turn right down the hill,
look both ways at that intersection where I almost got hit by a car
(my fault). back in high school, I ran track in the mornings
and went to dragon boat practice after class. now if I have the energy to run
after work it's a miracle, and that's okay because any run is a good run
and I am doing my best. I never feel more like a white woman girlboss
than when I am wearing a lavender hat and a running vest I don't need
for a 5K jog. someone has placed fresh flowers on every bench in this park
with a memorial plaque. stopping to cry about park bench flowers
is not very girlboss of me but Sandra was a loving mother and wife
and she's not here anymore, so I do it anyway. I wonder what my plaque
would say. *loving mother and wife and ran a sub-2-hour half-marathon*, maybe.
Sabrina Carpenter is singing about "me espresso" and it's not great crying music
so I start running again. after I'm gone, I hope someone loves me enough
to buy a plaque, and flowers every once in a while. how hard is it really?
I write cards for my coworkers every Christmas and see my family on the weekends.
someone will miss me. someone has to. I bet Sandra saved kittens from trees
and baked cookies for the neighbourhood and her kids called her their best friend.
one foot after another, all the way home. post activity to Strava. you go, girlboss.
show them what you're worth.

P.S.

I'm so happy for you. in another life
we got married and never had kids.
congratulations on your engagement!!!
I don't hate you, I'm just bad at texting.
I regret what I said the last time we spoke.
I still check your blog to see what you've been up to.
we wouldn't have worked, but I wish we had tried anyway.
is Toronto everything you wanted?
we were too young to know better.
I'm sad that I hurt you, but not sorry we stopped talking.
I appreciate the apology, but I needed it four years ago.
I kept all those emails we sent back in high school.
was I the reason you left?
you're the only one I can't write poems about.
if you phone me on New Year's Eve, I'll let it go to voicemail
and then call you back.
you made me who I am.
you made me who I'm not.
I am trying to be grateful for everything you gave me.
sincerely,
yours always,
take care,
all the best,

Ode to Commas

after Julie Mannell

    my lines are long   meandering   melt into each other   like sand
not declarative   confident   enough
    I learned shame   in fifth grade   dropping quarters in the slouch jar
while Mrs. McCusker told us
                        about her neighbour   a farmer
    who bent until his spine
                  stuck that way   she said he looked at the ground
forever what   does that say about the girls
                          who learned early that small is safer
   "sorry" is safer
                  girls who celebrate getting home alive
  or a pleasant first date
             who believe we owe this world   so much more

      than it's given us

                             I learned tenderness

  from the girl across the bar
                  who didn't know me
                        but asked if I was okay

            learned

to lower myself   pat poetry into the dirt   grow it like

ivy: tangled
        curled inwards
                     held upright   by a trellis of hands
  offering hugs
      tampons
         sticks of gum
                    a place to build

All This to Say

when you want something badly enough,
it turns your stomach to coiled muscle.

when my hunger clenches this desperately
I am surprised blood does not pour

from my eyes, surprised always at how my body
protects me from the animal of itself.

I cried in the bathtub, on the bus,
in the Starbucks on Granville while strangers stared

but said nothing; I am that same stranger
who stares, sips my latte in silence.

I place Amazon orders, buy spinach in bulk,
bring a reusable mug to save ten cents.

I forget my reusable mug.
wax poetic while taking out the garbage.

an ocean away, the earth continues her burning.
I feel her clenching in on us,

protecting herself from these animals she carries,
our need for green numbers, upwards arrows.

this brave new world, polished too bright.

all this to say that in the end, the last of us will run like blood
into her emptying stomach, her oceans, that maybe we deserved it,

that if we were kinder we might be worth
saving. I don't believe these words

but feel them in my gut like instinct, like an animal,
like a tide slowly rising

until it finally – blessedly –
sweeps me away.

May 13

push the door shut, click the lock into place
and I'm alone again, in the kitchen,
in the dark. after all this time, I should
be used to it: roommates, different cities,
one of us leaving at the end of the night. today, though,
it's too much to endure. that you were here
and now you're not. I don't remember
the first moment I knew that I loved you,
but it must have been something like this –
you, turning to walk out the door. my heart,
getting up to go with you.

2024, in Texts from My Sister

I need to stop writing fanfic doomsday scenarios about my own life.
I'm sure it'll be fine. like it is not that serious!!
I truly wish the best for her. it's so hard to be a girl.
it could be a spectacular failure but I love doing things as a bit.
it's easy to feel like nothing good is happening in the world,
but in reality we are joined by millions of people who are doing what they can.
I made u a playlist, hopefully it helps!!
honestly, that's kind of slay. probably the equivalent of hitting a blunt
(I've never done drugs before, I have no idea what hitting a blunt is like)
idk if you've seen but I can kinda see the northern lights from where I am! woooow!!!!!
I take back every time I said I was the funny one, clearly that crown should go to you.
we really only have each other out here.
we'll come back tomorrow with a renewed sense of purpose & drive.
there are kids in Palestine right now laughing and playing with each other.
I SAID I LOVE YOU!!!
we keep going until we don't anymore.

If Mary Can Do It

I give myself permission to write
about the small things. a trip
to the ice rink. the bus ride home.
cherry blossoms in full bloom. anything to feel
like I have anything at all to say.
my pen pal in Tokyo writes a book
and I find out through Twitter. it's getting easier
to see the future. marriage and a kid,
two probably, unless I change my mind. I want
people to remember me. I want to write like she did.
focused, intentional, whole poems taken over by a flock of starlings
or a blade of grass. not this wild tangle of thoughts
all pressed in together. I would blame
the internet, but I think it's just me. I want
to stop living through late-stage capitalism.
I want to do something about it
but without getting in trouble. I don't care
what you say – I need to be good. tell me
about despair, Mary. tell me if, at the end,
you felt you had done more
than just visit.

I Tour You Up East Hastings, from Nanaimo

okay! sooo that's my little garden suite – we don't get a lot of light, but at least it stays cool in the summer and the landlord is nice and we finally got rid of the spiders. I shouldn't buy groceries at Donald's, everything there is expensive, but it's convenient so I do. Jasper and I had dinner for the first time in a long time at Bai Bua Thai and she walked me home in the dead of winter. when I first moved here, It's Okay was this vegan place called Bad Apple and I recommended their waffle fries to anyone who would listen. I hope London Drugs will be done renovations soon because it was the closest place to get toilet paper. Iron Dog Books is the best and I should really visit more. one time I accidentally ordered pickup instead of delivery and Chimie and I had to walk to Chatime at like 9:00 p.m. to get our bubble tea. Mez bought coffee for a man named John at the McDonald's before we drove him to a warming centre. not everyone sees this city the way that I do. there are more empty storefronts than I remember. more construction sites, too. I think the new ones are apartment complexes. homes, I mean. I meet Mallory at Cup & Bun. what is home? I get my blood tested at LifeLabs. how can this be home? I order dinner from Sfinaki. everything is stolen land and I am cashing in. I buy bean sprouts and tamari paste at Sungiven Foods and speak english with the cashier. even if I wanted to, where would I go? the fire station and Anton's and the funeral parlour. John has two daughters he wishes he could see more. the canadian flag hanging outside Legion 148. an average house in this neighbourhood costs well over a million. we don't get a lot of light, but at least the landlord is nice. we don't get a lot of light but at least we have a landlord. we don't get a lot of light but.

Girl Camping

after Natasha Ramoutar

we pack five of us into the SUV, blast
"Total Eclipse of the Heart" so loud
it shakes the car –
and that, we decide,
is girl driving.

girl dinner is half a sandwich and a full chocolate cake
at 8:00 p.m. around the picnic table. I hand out
plastic cups that start melting when we fill them with hot chocolate
but girl camping means nothing can go wrong,
so we make it work.

we go girl hiking, which is regular hiking but better,
make friends with a cat at a bookstore,
buy borscht at the farmers' market,
drag our sleeping bags to the beach
and whisper secrets to the wind
as a meteor shower starts above us.

I decide we can speak about joy for once.
I decide that we are the joy.
Kirsten points out a shooting star
and everyone catches it except me.
Jackie tells a joke and I start laughing,
we are all laughing, everyone is laughing
as we do girl math into the morning:
two nights at a campsite plus a ferry, gas and food
divided by the most beautiful sunset in the world,
a dash of delirium from not enough sleep,
curry udon eaten out of paper bowls,
gratitude that stretches from horizon to horizon –
a return on investment so large

that it spills out of me into the night sky
and suspends time for just a moment
as we sit on the beach, still laughing,
making every second count.

June 27, Again and Again and Again

i.
I lift my head from your chest
on a lazy Sunday afternoon
and ask if you think you will ever get bored of me.

I'm not insecure like I used to be –
worked on my self-esteem and got off those Reddit forums
where everyone's cheating on each other all the time.

but it must happen eventually, right?
you sit straight up, look me in the eyes, say *how could you even ask*
and I hear the wind chime again,
loud and ringing, drowning out the doubt.

what an odd thing, for someone else
to know everything about you
and still want to be by your side.

ii.
we become plant parents on a whim
and now your apartment is a greenhouse.
we research obsessively: plants that are hard to kill,
don't need too much water, do well in low light.
we give them names: Persephone, Ophelia,
Young Theodore, Lil' Lep.
every morning, a small joy
to call ours: new bud,
leaf unfurled, roots taking hold,
stronger and taller
than the day before.

iii.
you bring water. you make dinner.
you encourage me to play video games
on the couch all day.
you go to the store
for tampons and ginger ale. you listen.
you wipe my tears. you drive me
everywhere. you hold my hand.
you kiss my forehead. you love me
so hard it feels impossible. you tell me
I'm beautiful and I finally believe you.

Elegy for Opportunity V

The last time Opportunity communicated with Earth was June 10, 2018.

hi, Oppy.

it's been a while, hey?
I'm not sure why I'm writing.
I need a good listener, I guess.

                    sorry, that sounded bad.
                    I hope you're doing okay.

                                      so.

I've been thinking a lot about kids.

whether I want them and all that.
TikTok keeps showing me all these cute babies and I think it's messing with my head –

yeah, yeah. I finally gave in and downloaded TikTok. I know.

but we've been talking about it more,
our future child – future children – and stuff.

I guess you wouldn't know anything about that.

                                                            sorry, I –

                I mean, you couldn't have kids
                but you knew people with kids,

                                    right? you must have. at NASA.

right. it's just –

it's just, I owe you an apology.
the last time we talked,
I was angry and scared,
and I was mean. I'm sorry.

                                                          Oppy,

things are bad right now.
really bad.

the world feels unrepairable.

unchecked greed and exploitation.
heat domes and cold snaps.
bombs, disease, starvation, genocide –
40,000 dead in Gaza.

                                        40,000.

                              I was going to list more things but I can't.
                              that one made me so sad. I don't know.

          Oppy, baby,
          I need you to tell me we are worth saving.

        but you won't, because you can't,
                                      because we killed you.

yesterday a little fly landed in the sink while I was washing my hands
and I watched it drown. didn't move a muscle. felt glad, even.

I wanted it dead.

        is that how you felt

about us by the end?

                                          I would if I were you.

    we abandoned you, Oppy.

I guess I don't know
where we go from here –

                        what if I have a baby?

          what if I have a baby
                    and the world ends while she's still in it?

    Oppy, I have to tell you something.
    I didn't know you until after you died.

all these poems, these have just been for me.
they have the whole time.

I write poetry
because I need someone to tell me
that it's going to be okay.

even if that someone is
                                      me.

                                      even if I'm lying through my teeth.

I'm tired, Oppy.
you were tired too, at the end, weren't you,
when the dust came

                                      and it all went quiet?

I think I would be a good mom
if I got the chance.

I would love that kid so much,
like no one has ever loved a kid before
                                      and I would read to her every night
                                      and sing her lullabies
                                      and teach her everything I know

                                      and it wouldn't be enough
                                      but I would try, I would try so hard

    and I would tell her about you, of course.
    the little Mars rover that could.

you were extraordinary, you know.
lasted sixty times longer than you were supposed to
found evidence of water on Mars
took a bajillion photos

        you made the rest of us look bad, really.
        you overachiever, you.

the valley you're sitting in,
they named it after you.
Perseverance.
you never gave up.

well.

thanks for listening, Oppy.
can I sing you something?
what's that one they played you, the last song –

oh. I know.
I know. it's time.
I will. I'll –

yes. whatever happens,
                     I promise.

                                     I love you very much.
                                     good night.

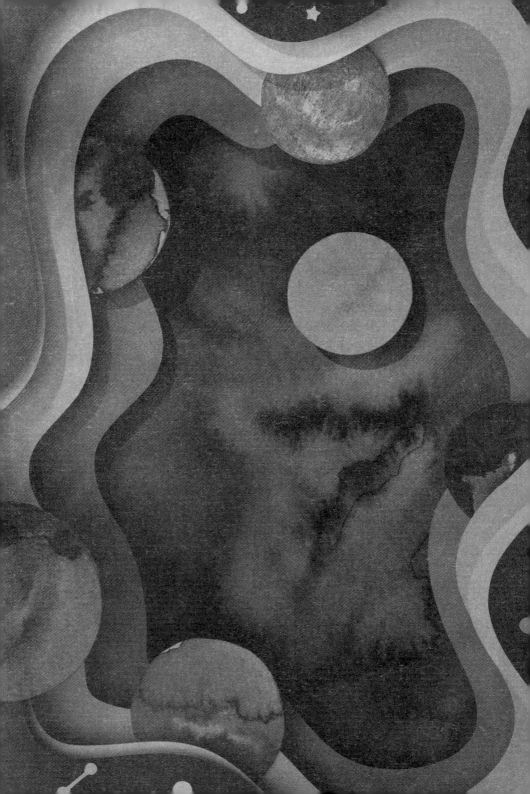

Notes on the Poems

Versions of the poems in this manuscript first appeared in my chapbook *arrhythmia* (Rahila's Ghost Press, 2022), and in books and journals including *Honey & Lime*, *Room* magazine, *PRISM international*, *talking about strawberries all of the time*, *The /tƐmz/ Review*, *Parentheses*, *Maisonneuve*, *Canthius*, *Augur* magazine, *Watch Your Head: Writers and Artists Respond to the Climate Crisis* (Coach House Books, 2020) and *Quarandreams: A Reflection of the Pandemic Through Photography and Poetry* (2022). Thank you to all of these publications for their support of my work.

"**August 7**" references Ocean Vuong's poem "Nothing."

"**Elegy for Opportunity**" borrows the lines "there is nothing lonelier / than the little Mars rover" from Matthew Rohrer's poem "There Is Absolutely Nothing Lonelier."

"**On Bouldering**" borrows its concept and several lines from Terrence Abrahams' poem "on amateur geology."

"**Say Goodbye Like You Mean It**" borrows its title from a lyric in "Stop Making This Hurt" by Bleachers.

"**Elegy for Opportunity II, as Museum Timeline**" cites a number of sources:

1. Jasper Planetarium, "Telescope Experience," Tourism Jasper, https://www.jasper.travel/experiences/telescope-experience/.
2. "Jasper's History," Tourism Jasper, https://www.jasper.travel/discover-jasper/jaspers-story/.
3. "Cultural Use Area," Government of Canada, August 1, 2023, https://parks.canada.ca/pn-np/ab/jasper/autochtones-indigenous/aca-cua.
4. "Girl with Dreams Names Mars Rovers 'Spirit' and 'Opportunity,'" NASA Jet Propulsion Laboratory, June 8, 2003, https://www.jpl.nasa.gov/news/girl-with-dreams-names-mars-rovers-spirit-and-opportunity/.

5   Diane Selkirk, "Jasper National Park Drove Indigenous People from Their Land. Now They're Coming Home," *Montecristo*, April 15, 2024, https://montecristomagazine.com/magazine/volume-17/jasper-national-park-drove-indigenous-people-land-now-theyre-coming-home.

6   @confusedhamster2826, comment on "NASA Says Goodbye to Mars Rover Opportunity after 15 Years," CNET, February 13, 2019, video, 2:33, https://www.youtube.com/watch?v=VwNvSYgne8c.

"**So I Played 100 Hours of Video Games This Month**" makes several references to Supergiant Games' *Hades*, one of the best video games of all time, and one that you should definitely play if you haven't yet.

"**Winter in Ottawa**" borrows several lines from a blog post published on *Open Book* by Manahil Bandukwala titled "Poetry as Joy: A Retrospective and Introduction."

"**The Science of Holding On**" references an article published in *Newsweek* by Gaurav Khanna titled "Time Travel Is Technically Possible – But We Need an Object with Infinite Mass."

"**17 Inspiring Brand Manifestos as Compiled by Chris Getman**" is a found poem compiled of lines from a blog post published on Agency Arsenal by Chris Getman titled "17 Inspiring Brand Manifestos."

"**Chief Editor of** *The Moon News*" borrows the concept of a pun war from Sarah Kay's poem "Table Games."

"**Six Months and Counting**" borrows the line "they say there are still good people in the world" from Isabella Wang's poem "Late."

"**The Big Breakup (Taylor's Version)**" references several songs by Taylor Swift, including "invisible string," "Labyrinth," "mirrorball" and "Bejeweled."

"I've Started Running Half-Marathons Like Everyone Else" was inspired by a TikTok from Michael Aldag (@michael.aldag) about how I'm not special and everyone does this when they approach thirty, apparently.

"Ode to Commas" was inspired by a Tweet from poet Julie Mannell (@juliemannell): "I hate commas. A comma is just a period without a backbone."

"If Mary Can Do It" references several poems by Mary Oliver, including "Starlings in Winter," "Wild Geese" and "When Death Comes."

"Girl Camping" borrows several lines and concepts from Natasha Ramoutar's poem "Like Makeshift Crowns."

"Elegy for Opportunity V" contains a death toll that has needed to be updated several times, with substantial and horrifying increases each time, during the writing of this manuscript. By the time you read this it will be out of date. Free Palestine, now and always.

Acknowledgements

To Natasha, the most incredible editor and poetic partner I could have asked for: this book is yours too. Thank you for sending that first query email, for keeping me organized, for your insightful questions and suggestions and for nerding out with me over *Hades* and *Baldur's Gate 3* and all of our identical cultural touchpoints. The vibes are, and always will be, immaculate.

To the Wolsak & Wynn team – Paul, Noelle, Ashley and Jennifer – thank you for taking a chance on this book. I have felt so supported and cared for through every step of this process, and I'm honoured that my debut book is from Wolsak & Wynn.

To Kilby, for the beautiful cover art and book design: thank you for capturing the essence of this book so perfectly!

To Mallory, Curtis and Brandi: this book was only made possible by the chapbook that came before it. Thank you for the gift of Rahila's Ghost Press and for helping me take my first steps into the publishing world with *arrhythmia*.

To Mallory again, for editing an early version of this manuscript: thank you for believing that my little package of poems could be a book one day. You have been so generous with your time and energy and I am eternally grateful.

To Chimie: I miss you all the time. Thank you for reading early drafts of this manuscript, for inspiring several of its poems and for always calling me the most beautiful woman in the world. And sorry again for killing your plant.

To Tina: more than ten years later, we're still out here doing the thing! Thank you for being my first and favourite writing buddy, for sticking with me through hours of revisions at La Forêt and for your endless support and enthusiasm. I am so proud of you and can't wait for your poems to take the world by storm.

To Isabella, Steve, the Food & Friends Club, the Love Poems Collective, the SFU English department and all the writers and editors who have told me that my voice is important: I would not still be doing this without you. Thank you for showing me how writing can open up possibilities for a better world.

To my friends: so many of you are featured in these poems, and each of you has supported and inspired my work in different ways. Thanks for all the meals and laughter and board game nights and for not holding it against me when I forget to respond to your texts.

To Mom, Dad, Amanda and my family: thank you for raising me to believe that I could do anything I wanted to. These poems are full of so much love, and I learned that from you first.

To Opportunity: thank you for offering me a way to think through love, grief and our obligations to each other. I wish we had been better to you. I hope we will learn from our mistakes.

To Mesbah: the poems have said it all. I love you and I always will.

And to you, the reader: thank you for spending time with these poems. I hope that they met you where you are and sat with you awhile. I'll keep the fire going. Stay as long as you need.

Natalie Lim is a Chinese-Canadian poet living on the unceded, traditional territories of the Musqueam, Squamish and Tsleil-Waututh Peoples (Vancouver, BC). She is the winner of the 2018 CBC Poetry Prize and *Room* magazine's 2020 Emerging Writer Award, with work published in *Arc Poetry Magazine*, *Best Canadian Poetry 2020* and elsewhere. She is the author of a chapbook, *arrhythmia* (Rahila's Ghost Press, 2022).